THE BROKEN TURTLE

This detail from a 1947 Ontario Department of Lands and Forests map of Algonquin Provincial Park (above) shows the area in which author Mark LaVigne canoed. Blackbear Lake, near the top of the map just left of centre, was renamed Tom Thomson Lake in 1958 to commemorate the famous artist, whose painting *In Algonquin Park* (1914–15) is reproduced below.

THE BROKEN TURTLE

Mark Hunter LaVigne

Rock's Mills Press
Oakville, Ontario
2021

Published by
Rock's Mills Press
www.rocksmillspress.com

Copyright © 2021 by Mark Hunter LaVigne.
All rights reserved. Published by arrangement with the author.

Frontispiece
Map detail: W.A. Barnard, cartographer. Map published by Ontario Department of Lands and Forests, 1947. Courtesy University of Toronto Libraries, Map and Data Library. Thomson painting: McMichael Canadian Art Collection/Wikimedia Commons.

Cover Image
Turtle: John Edwards Holbrook, 1842; from the book *North American Herpetology*

Cover and Interior Photos
Larry O'Donoghue, Ryan O'Donoghue and Mark Hunter LaVigne

For information, please contact Rock's Mills Press at
customer.service@rocksmillspress.com

Canoe Lake is one of those lakes in Algonquin Park that almost always is challenging. Maybe it's bad luck on my part, but during my twenty trips on it over the years the wind always seemed to be against me. On the way in-country, and on the outbound trip as well! Sometimes we've encountered three-foot swells. A few times, though, the lake was as calm as glass, even at midday when we always seem to hit the water.

When I say "we," I mean my usual gang: my best friend Larry, one or two of my kids, one or two of his kids, nephews, and friends. There have been other trips with neighbours and other friends. Even as an official guide—once.

In *The Broken Ukulele*, I described my solo backpacking trip not too far from this entry point. Part of the reason for the trip was to practise fitting all my gear into one pack, so that eventually I could go on a solo canoe trip. Well, after the Covid-19 lockdowns, I never *ever* want to be alone again!

So here I am, with what used to be small boys and what used to be a skinny, super-fit best friend. The boys are now mostly more than six feet tall and in their mid- to late twenties. My buddy is still quite fit, and me—well, worse off than when backpacking solo a few summers back. I can blame that on Covid too.

Entering the parking area at Canoe Lake, I had never seen so many cars! Lots of day trippers. And lots of people canoeing for the first time, or at least for the first time in many years. And not one U.S. licence plate. Tripping during Covid!

For one of the first times in memory, Canoe Lake was very calm. Not calm as glass, like it was the time I took my

Russian-Canadian neighbour for his first Algonquin canoe trip—but close. It was very busy with people trying out canoes for the first time, a normal occurrence, but sometimes challenging when we have a fully loaded canoe and have to make some emergency manoeuvres.

Once everyone gathered, seven of us in total, three separate vehicles, all from different parts of the GTA, we unloaded the cars, somehow all found parking spots, and loaded the canoes. We were off after some kibitzing.

It was late to depart even for us, about two-thirty in the afternoon. But the sky was clear, the wind minimal, the lake smooth.

Canoe tripping is different than backpacking. A canoe can carry several hundred pounds, including people. You are more open to the elements in many ways—wind, sun, rain—and lightning can kill you. Physically, it demands more upper-body strength, but if you have someone strong in the bow, and the canoe isn't overloaded, you can make progress. On a trip earlier this summer with my backcountry buddy John, we used extended kayak paddles. *Now that's the way to do it!* First ear worm of the trip. Dire Straits. MTV.

Backpacking essentially takes you into the woods for a lot of your trip. At first the weight of your pack is daunting, but your body gets used to it, as it does to paddling on a canoe trip. Your mind can go on autopilot walking or paddling. When you meld with the canoe, it becomes an amazing extension of your body. I feel most embraced by Mother Earth when I am in a canoe. But being in the forest fulltime reinvigorates me. I only became conscious in my forties of the energy that trees give off. On a backpacking trip, you are in the woods fulltime, not just sleeping there.

Within twenty minutes we were almost between Wapomeo and Cook Islands. We passed the northern tip of Gilmour Island, where the great Canadian painter Tom Thomson's body was found. That is also where we took shelter during a horrible white water experience on our first trip with our oldest kids, Amalee and Ryan. "Paddle or die!" Of all the stupid dad-things to say to an 11-year-old daughter in a three-foot swell when she is terrified in the bow! Earlier I'd told her to forget about the canoe if it flipped, swim to me, and we would get to the nearby shore together. Needless to say, she did not come on another Algonquin canoe trip for a few years!

We passed Camp Wapomeo, eerily silent during this Time of Covid. Usually there are swimmers and boats and lots of happy noise emanating from the place. This time nothing but seagulls.

After Wapomeo, the winds usually pick up, but not this time. We passed the townsite of Mowat to the left, now a cluster of cottages, behind which, kept secret, deep in the bush, is a graveyard where it's now believed Tom Thomson was buried. On the other side of the lake is the day-tripper tourist attraction—Tom Thomson's cairn and totem pole. Worth a visit once maybe. But usually we just want to get to our camping spot!

At the top end of Canoe Lake, two women were sitting in their canoe confused by a sign pointing one way to Potter Creek and the other to Joe Lake. We asked where they were going. One said Joe Lake. "We are heading that way. It is up here—you can follow if you like." One woman asked, "Are you sure?" We nodded and kept going. Obviously, my son and I were not trustworthy-looking enough! The other two canoes in our party told them the same thing and got the same response. I wonder if they ever made it.

On canoe trips, and at portages, it is always nice to share information about vacant sites or the weather ahead. The idea is to be pleasant but respectful of people's privacy and to lend a helping hand if needed.

We turned to the right at the junction and noticed the water was a bit lower than usual. Past a few of the grandfathered cottages on long term leases back to the park, and then up a small river to the right to avoid the long portage. Yes, we practice "portage avoidance techniques" when we can.

One year we dragged our canoes up a small creek bed. Another time over a large beaver dam. This sort of thing is always risky for the canoe and can be damaging to the environment. But we still go up this small river, to cut the portage to only a few hundred yards.

A few passes through the portage and we were all gathered, loaded and ready to go, snacking a little, all of us seemingly lost in our own thoughts.

Portages are historically important places. Generally human-made, they are often at the confluence of different rivers, where villages, towns and even cities grew up. Or, as in this case, they are located on higher elevations between lakes. The portage between Canoe Lake and Joe Lake has a dam, one of many throughout Algonquin to control water levels. Over this dam went Tom Thomson's body after he drowned.

After a half-hour break we were on our way again, under the bridge carrying a road to Camp Arowhon on Teepee Lake. Then we are into Joe Lake proper, past Joe Island through the Western Gap where we could see Elephant Rock, one of the most sought-after campsites on this route. It is not far from where I saw what I believe was Tom Thomson's ghost.

It happened on the north side of the lake. Either deer or moose woke me up while munching near my tent. I walked out to the small point adjacent to our campsite and sat by the

water smoking. There was low-hanging fog. I noticed a shape coming from the left, not too far from Arowhon Lodge, a beautiful and quite expensive hotel on Little Joe Lake not far from this spot. For a few minutes I assumed it was a soloist who wanted to experience a canoe ride at two-thirty in the morning. Then I realized there was no sound. No sound of the paddle hitting the water or the gunnel, no sound of anything. Silence. The dark shape of a man, soloing mid-canoe, rather tall. Then he moved into a small bank of low-lying fog. And never emerged. A wind picked up, blowing the fog away shortly thereafter. No canoe. A chill went down my spine. I headed back to the tent and my sleeping sons. I did not fall back to sleep for quite a while.

I have mentioned Tom Thomson a few times now. The legend. The great Canadian artist, who inspired the formation of the Group of Seven. Journalist Roy MacGregor has written four superb books on Tom Thomson, one a novel entitled *Canoe Lake*, which I highly recommend. His fourth book—a superb work of nonfiction—put what happened to Tom to rest, more or less.

Thomson drowned on Joe Lake. He was found some days later washed ashore on the aforementioned island in Canoe

Lake, fishing line wrapped around one leg. Somehow Tom had a hole punched in his skull, perhaps from a fireplace poker. It is presumed he died of a cerebral hemorrhage and then drowned. His body is believed now to be buried west of Canoe Lake. In his relatively short life he painted some of the most beloved and significant works of Canadian art. It is wonderful to paddle the same waters he did and see the same landscape. I recommend all of MacGregor's books and thank him so much for his scholarship and also for being supportive of some of my own ventures. You can see some of Thomson's work at the fantastic McMichael gallery north of Toronto. The collection at the Art Gallery of Ontario is also superb.

Not far from my ghost sighting is another campsite where we had stayed on our very first night in the park so many years ago. After getting our tents set up and the fire started, I heard Ryan shout. Amalee screamed. I ran after her, telling her to slow down since she was heading for a small cliff at the lake's edge—and promptly and very badly twisted my ankle on a root. I hobbled to where the kids were. A huge snapping turtle was near shore, mesmerizing them. I immediately soaked my ankle in the cold water. The next day we were in cold water a lot of the time avoiding portages, which helped my ankle immensely. After getting back to the city my doctor said I had broken a few small bones in there. I have carried tensor bandages on camping trips ever since!

We now pushed up through another part of the Oxtongue Rver and into Teepee Lake past Camp Arowhon. It was also Covid quiet! Usually this lake is filled with sailboats. The large camp always emits a cacophony of happy camper sounds, the schedule bell ringing. Now absolutely silent. Eerie!

At the north end of Teepee Lake one always feels a strong current coming toward you, flowing down towards the dam and into Canoe Lake. The current was still there. We moved to the eastern shore to avoid the current and pushed onward.

At another gap, I remembered a night during my first "official" guiding role, with two priests in training and a renowned film maker. That outing was a late September trip to help prepare key messaging, on-camera, for a major project that was to launch the following spring. The project would see a group of thirty young Jesuits, Indigenous people, and other individuals paddle 900 kilometres up Georgian Bay, across the French River, through Lake Nipissing, then down the Mattawa River to the Ottawa River and to Montreal, re-tracing the route taken by St. Jean de Brébeuf almost 400 years earlier.

On that trip, we planned to stay on Joe Lake, but disrespectful trippers had overbooked the lake. They didn't have permits allowing them to be there. We spent more than an hour of precious daylight looking for an empty campsite and ended up paddling north up the Oxtongue until we could find one. We did not land until nightfall, making our set-up, firewood gathering and dinner preparation difficult. When trippers camp on a lake illegally it forces others to do the same. Frankly, such practices can endanger others. That is why the fines are so high. Thankfully the weather was dry, albeit cold, so we survived and had a productive evening of fireside discussions about our project and fruitful work on key messaging the next day.

We paddled into a narrow channel, technically the Oxtongue River again, and then took a sharp turn to the left into Fawn Lake. To the right of the turn, there is a bay where we have seen moose doing their salad-bar thing. After passing through this tiny lake we were back into the Oxtongue for a short while and then into Littledoe Lake itself.

Some years ago in this spot, a song popped into my head, and so I started singing the first verse. Sean, one of Larry's sons, always remembers that song and asks for it, indeed asked for it again on this trip at our first campfire. Years later, it is finally finished as promised, Sean, and you'll find it on the next page.

If Larry's canoe is in the lead, he goes down the false entry to Tom Thomson Lake every time. But we were in the lead this trip, so went past the small unnamed island and then turned left into a small river.

To the right was the main entrance into Littledoe's eastern sections. The lake looks like a giant "M", and we have stayed on it several nights over the years.

I Canoe I Canoe I Canoe

C
I canoe the Ottawa
Am
I canoe through Mattawa
Dm F G
I canoe I canoe I canoe
(repeat same chords throughout)

Let the sun shine down
Let the winds be still
Let the loons call my name

I canoe to Nottawa
I canoe to Oshawa
I canoe I canoe I canoe

Let the sun shine down
Let the winds be still
Let the loons call my name

I canoe to Chippewa
I canoe by Arkansa
I canoe I canoe I canoe

Let the sun shine down
Let the winds be still
Let the loons call my name

Our left turn into Lily Pad Bay marks the spot where we once saw five moose at their salad bar, always a thrill. The kids were pretty young, and we side-paddled away from the potential canoe stompers.

Then to the beaver dam. One year it was so high we could not get the canoes past it. The boys were young and there was no easy way around on either side. We paddled back and had to stay on Littledoe's furthest flank, illegally, but we had no choice. This kind of situation is when it is permissible to do this. Of course, this is also when the wardens come by, but since we were straight up about it we were forgiven.

The wardens were likely responding to complaints about a very noisy campsite across that part of the lake. Well into the wee hours they partied, throwing glow sticks into the lake. The wardens told us they issued several tickets to them. But late on our last night we noticed two headlamps coming across the lake towards our site. At first, I thought it was a couple of those campers needing something, but it turned out to be two young women, seemingly in distress. It turned out they had started a root fire at the portage at the east end of our lake and needed to paddle to a phone at the camp, something we discouraged as being dangerous on such a dark night. We managed to get one bar on one of our cellphones and called the fire into the OPP. We then treated these two Americans to the last of our CC and Coke and played them

Canadian songs on my Martin backpacker guitar, which sent them to bed quite quickly. They left the next morning very early. Then the helicopter came shortly thereafter, dumping fire retardant on the root fire.

On another trip into Littledoe we snagged a beautiful site on a point. Suddenly, in the late afternoon, there was shouting at the end of the lake. A flare shot into the sky. In the backcountry, this is a very serious call for help. Ryan, Sean, and I dashed into the canoe and sped toward the campsite where the flare had been fired from. At least two other canoes were converging on the site too. Then we noticed another canoe paddling away from the site frantically, towards a bay that did not have a portage or exit river. They came back. One young man was in the front, face white as a sheet, and the story came out. They were doing magic mushrooms and the young man was having an anaphylactic episode.

At this moment, thunder and lightning suddenly erupted to the west. Sometimes storms move through this area very quickly, seemingly blowing up out of nowhere, usually coming from Georgian Bay. We guided them in the correct direction past our campsite and around the bend into the main channel. A woman came down to the shore from her campsite identifying herself as a nurse. One look at the young man and she asked what he had taken. The storm was now upon us. We all advised the guys not to attempt to make it to the camp and resident doctor stationed there—not in a thunderstorm. But they pushed on. Ryan, Sean, and I made it back to our site just in time. Ducking under the tarp Larry and Sean were holding up, we all cowered there as the storm raged through.

Returning from Littledoe memory lane, this trip all three of our canoes went over the beaver dam without incident. A little bit of effort, but not bad compared to other years.

Keegan and I had a light canoe. We brought one pack each, and water, and a full wet sack of tetra pack wine, and one folding camp chair. So, we were lighter than usual. We left the aluminum table in the car. Indeed, my backpacking trips got me into the habit of carrying just one pack and he now follows suit!

I remembered yet another story from times past.

My Russian Canadian neighbour, Sergei, and I came through here once about mid-September. Just as we reached the gap in the beaver dam, Sergei jumped out of the bow and a beaver came running at him, whacking its tail and making munching noises. Sergei looked at me and said, "That very big rat." I laughed so hard. "It's a beaver, Sergei, and he is not too happy." Thankfully the beaver went back to the shore and disappeared under the dam into his den.

Once again, we were paddling among lily pads with a canoe route carved through them. Another bay loomed, where we had seen moose before at their salad bar.

The first site we came to was the one where Sergei and I stayed some years ago. I shot my best picture of all that I've taken on my Algonquin trips; the light was reflected off my old red canoe. Luckily, I had the camera handy in my lifejacket and quickly snapped the photo. The sunset lasted only a minute or so and I was able to catch it. My luckiest shot ever. (You can see it on the next page.)

By this point in the trip, I am almost always running out of gas. This is when someone pushes ahead to try to snag the island site. We have only managed to stay there once over all

the years. It is like winning the lottery. It is a flat site with a beach and a cliff to the west side that is perfect for a sundown gathering, and for cliff-jumping as well, though one must always be very, very careful. The first come, first served policy of the park always makes it a bit of a crap shoot when one wants the best site on a lake, and it seems every lake we have been on has one!

Algonquin Park is sometimes known for its visitors with naturist tendencies. Our one time at the island site we had finished breakfast and clean-up and were about to go swimming when two women pulled up in a canoe at the small island about 200 yards away from ours. They then removed their bathing suits, went swimming and began sunning themselves. Another time years ago, when the boys were quite small, a young family pulled up at Elephant Rock across from our site on Joe Lake and promptly stripped down to nothing to go swimming. A bit shocking both times, but we are fine with it!

Often, I worry there will be no sites left. "Site anxiety" I call it—SA for short. It only hits me when I get to the lake for which we have a permit. And Tom Thomson Lake, formerly called Blackbear Lake because of the very smart black bears on its east side, is a main canoe thoroughfare. Like a canoe 401. The purists hate it. It has three portages on it, so it generally gets lots of traffic. But I love it; there are so many nooks and crannies and so many memories.

Once when we came into the lake the northern sky turned dark green, with red lightning flashing out of it. (This was also when the boys were quite young.) Every site on the east side was taken. We finally got to the most northerly site, which was thankfully vacant because of all the goose poo.

(On the way up Tom Thomson Lake that trip, a new song popped into my head. It eventually turned into "Rain Rain" with my old band, the Coyotes).

We landed the canoes, Larry and I constantly looking up at the menacing sky. We quickly unpacked the canoes and set up the tents while we had the boys—five of them, our sons and Larry's nephew Jason on his first canoe trip—scoop up the goose poo with canoe paddles and move it to the edges of the site. I have never seen so much goose poo in my life except on the Toronto Islands!

Then we got dinner going. Just as we were all fed and cleaned up and settling into some guitar playing by the campfire, the storm hit. Suddenly the temperature dropped at least ten degrees. We scrambled for our tents—Larry had set up two at the edge of the forest, I set mine up on the point by a small copse of trees on the campsite's north side. The trees were a bit higher than our tent, protecting us from the fierce winds and lightning. There was an old burnt tree on the south side of the campsite. I realized later it must once have been hit by lightning. Maybe not the best place to pitch a tent? But I was worried about trees in the forest blowing down. This storm was the strongest I'd ever seen in the park.

In my tent my boys were already asleep. I had placed our equipment and clothing barrels in the corners of the tent. I always put my sleeping bag in between the boys so I could cuddle them somewhat during storms and animal visits, and that is what I did this time, thinking we might be blown off the point or hit by lightning. Weirdly enough, the storm was coming from the north. And sometimes the wind was blowing from all directions, with huge blasts of thunder and immensely bright lightning. Close to dawn, the storm finally passed. I got out of the tent to take a pee. Larry heard me and came out too. We could see that everything had stayed put, including the canoes and paddles and the lifejackets underneath. Thankful to be alive, I went back to sleep. We all slept in that morning until about eleven. That storm actually spawned tornadoes to the east, and some trees fell on campers in the north part of the park, killing two!

Back to the present. Keegan and I headed towards the island. Jason, Jean Paul and Ryan were already there. Then we saw it. A single tent, with no one visible! Urghh. We paddled around the island. It took a while to get to the second site, which the other guys didn't like much. Dark and dreary.

"We should just follow Larry," my son said. Larry by now was across the lake exploring the final bay before the portage entrance. Larry usually chooses the site; it is his Type A Capricorn way. I am more a Type B Capricorn, but that is because I was born two months premature. My "go to" excuse!

We passed another site adjacent to the island where we stayed years ago. That is where we'd met Crackle, the friendliest turtle in the world.

Crackle was a young snapping turtle who hung out with

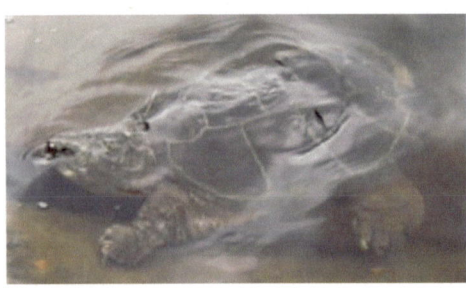

us for four days. He had a hatchet wound in his shell. Some terrible people tried to kill him, either scared by him, although he was small and very friendly, or for food. I hate to think that black marketeers were in our beloved park!

He came out of the water and moved his head in time to my guitar playing. The kids loved him. My sons Hunter and Keegan and Larry's sons Ryan and Sean fed Crackle our leftover eggs from breakfast, and played with him with sticks, which he liked to bite.

He even let me swim with him underwater, testing my client's new underwater camera. Now if I could only find that video in my mess of a computer archive!

When we got back from that trip, I reported him to Algonquin Park animal rescue. They did rescue him, repaired his shell, and released him a month later back into the lake. They were wonderful and so proactive in reaching out to me, letting us know that Crackle—that's what the kids had named him—was safe and back home in his hatch lake.

Last June, we were on the same lake with my eldest

daughter, my British cousin's husband (it was lifelong dream of his to go on an Algonquin canoe trip), and some other friends. Guess who came to visit us? Man, Crackle had grown. But still friendly, he raised his head out of the water and I swear he recognized me!

My daughter Amalee was thrilled. The turtle is her spirit animal. And my cousin Paul, despite his mosquito and deer fly bites, was also mesmerized. Poor Paul, there are hardly any mosquitoes in London, England, and despite the Deet 40 spray we gave him, he got bitten from his hat line to his boot tops. Of course, it *was* early June in the park, prime bug season, but that was the only opening they had in their travel itinerary so that is when we went. And I forgot the bug nets. Our companions, Ian and Rene, had an extra for my daughter. But poor Paul, poor Paul, poor Paul. Me, I let them bite me until now they do not bite me anymore. Plus, I believe copious wine consumption helps stave them away too!

The turtle we saw this trip was much larger, but with the same hatchet scar in his shell. By comparing photos, we confirmed afterwards it was indeed Crackle. And I swear he remembered me. We only found him on our last morning there as we were packing up, so we did not have a long visit with him. Amalee did spend some time with him while Paul and I loaded our canoe. That turtle encounter made her trip! She had not been on this lake for at least sixteen years, and this was only her third canoe trip with me. (The trip before, at the very south end of the park with her and my son Keegan, I forgot all of the plates and utensils, not to mention the peanut butter, butter and ketchup. I also dropped my glasses in the water. Miraculously she found them!)

On this new trip, my canoe "non-solo" (I will say it once more: after Covid, I never want to be alone again!) into Tom Thomson Lake, I was really hoping Crackle would hear my music and track me down wherever we found a campsite.

And so we went into the last hard paddle, exhausted. Sore butt (forgot the seat pads). Thirsty, out of water. Hot, needing a swim. Sore shoulders, a reminder to go to the gym or lift those small weights under my desk more often. Sore abs, the same.

Larry was signalling us. But we could not tell if his swinging his paddle overhead meant "Keep coming" or "Stop coming, the site is taken." We kept coming. Larry and his son Sean were parked and unloading when we got there. They had decided to stay, thank God, because I could not paddle another stroke!

(You may be wondering why we didn't have walkie-talkies. Well, we brought them on past trips and wrecked two sets in rain storms or by dropping them into the water.)

We got ashore, and I popped open a wine tetra pak. And we toasted yet another hard paddle into my favourite lake in the park—and down memory lane.

Our big boys are veteran backcountry canoers now, so everyone knew what to do. All the packs were lugged up from the canoe landing, sleeping sites claimed and tents set up. I helped Keegan with my backpacking tent, supposedly a two-person tent but really only for 1½ people! I then carried the toilet seat up to the thunder box. I have been doing this for years—ever since I got a splinter sitting on such a box, which has a toilet seat hole cut in the wooden top that covers the pit beneath. Makes it more comfortable. I often forget the toilet seat when we leave and have wondered from time to time what happens to all of them! Reminds me of the one we found at a thunder box on the Western Uplands Trail, but that one had a lid, was screwed down and greeted visitors with a Sharpie note from "Ed." (You'll find a picture of it in my book *The Broken Ukulele*.)

We finished getting the camp set up and had begun meal prep when Keegan noticed three canoes approaching. Young guys, quite lost, asking about a lake that was four portages away. Then Keegan realized they were older brothers of high school friends from our town, and that they were quite wasted. It was coming up on five o'clock in the afternoon, so it was doubtful they would make it to their destination. However, they didn't seem to care. I showed them my map and off they went. The lead canoe headed in the correct direction, the other two the wrong way, finally correcting after some yelling from the lead canoe.

Jason and Keegan called out to me: "Dad, that might be the turtle!" I had been nattering on for some time about Crackle revisiting us the summer before and there he was. Head sticking up out of the water about fifty yards offshore. I called out "Crackle!" very happily. Then Jason did the unimaginable! He threw a rock at him, fortunately missing, and Crackle submerged.

"What are you doing?" I asked.

Jason, a brilliant engineer, replied, "I thought it was a log. Just testing."

Crackle, who'd come to see me, was gone. So was the marketability of this book, movie rights, fame and fortune! I then caught Jason sending his fishing lure out. "I am trying to lure him in." Not a chance Crackle would visit us *ever* again!

Later that afternoon we did see him again near the little island in front of us. But he never came back to the campsite. Now Hollywood will not be interested for sure, I thought to myself.

Then I finally went for a swim. Canoe tripping for guys like Larry and me means we can be our ADD selves, always busy, with no Post-it notes to keep us on track, but eventually we need to cool off. I went for a swim, then came out to the clothesline to get my towel. A little black microfleece one. It was *gone*. After some inquiries, Jason admitted to using it to clean up the kitchen mess, thinking it was a dish towel. Are you seeing the pattern now? Kidding! Jason is one of the nicest people I have ever met. He has been so grateful we have taken him on these trips. He has grown into a lovely young man, hardworking, brilliant. But I am *not* going to ask him to be my agent on the dreamed-about turtle movie, that's for sure!

Keegan came and asked for my backcountry fishing kit. He opened up the package. "Dad, there are no rods in here." I forgot to check before packing it. And then I thought to myself, "Was it Jason who broke the rod some years ago?" Again, just kidding. Somehow, the rods were misplaced. I have to remember to try and find some replacement rods. There are Post-it notes for that.

What would time in the backcountry be for me without an earworm? Today's was "Sundown" by Gordon Lightfoot. Of course, the sheet music wasn't in the waterproof songbooks I brought along on the trip. That is the one sure way for me to get rid of an earworm—play it! I haven't learned this Lightfoot song. That would be remedied come fall.

Larry always brings kiln-dried baked hardwood for our first fire. The boys gathered dead wood for a big enough fire tonight, and tomorrow would be a full wood production day.

Our traditional steak dinner was planned for the next night, with Keegan helping Larry with the prep duties as he has always done on these trips since he was very little. He obviously drank too much wine because later that night I awoke in the tent with him outside being sick, poor kid. The other guys covered him with a tarp and actually cleaned up his mess for him. Good group of kids. Keegan needed some ibuprofen the next morning for sure.

I am always blown away the first night by how quiet this place is. The silence weighs on our urban-accustomed ear drums. It is pressing, enveloping. So far, I hadn't even heard a jet yet. There being a pandemic on, there were none! As the gloaming set in, the beauty of this place overwhelmed me yet again!

Dinner done and cleaned up, the party began. Well, it started when we landed really. I love this shot of us on the beach, looking at the water life with our headlamps, so happy to be in this place!

We woke up a little late the second day, but since I had gone to bed quite early—I always do on the first night after such a strenuous paddle—I was first up, first to the thunder box and then getting the coffee going. That aroma usually gets Larry up and then the rest awake in dribs and drabs.

We had a wonderful big breakfast. You can imagine with five young men in their twenties how much food gets eaten at each meal. As always, Larry and Sean took care of the meal planning and procurement—very grateful for that. My eldest daughter will never let me forget the time on a trip that I forgot the bag of dishes and utensils and condiments!

The day gently slid past. Time takes a back seat here. It slows down. Keegan and Larry and I took two canoes into the dead-end bay beside our campsite to harvest wood. We always try to find dead wood that is along the edge of the lakes, usually bone dry, and it helps the conservation of the lakes as well.

My backcountry buddy John, who came on the second backpacking trip I did on the Western Uplands Trail to ensure I had details correct for *The Broken Ukulele*, taught me a trick on our early summer canoe trip. Harvest the top wood off beaver dams! This wood is already free of bark and side limbs, usually bone dry having been baked in the sun, and manageable in size in both length and thickness—easy to cut up with a hand saw.

We managed to get a whole canoe load of beaver-prepared wood. When we got back to the campsite Sean, who had just finished a science degree, claimed the wood would be covered with beaver disease. Beaver fever! I doubted it, not after that long in the sun, but it did beg a good question. The boys went to work prepping all of the firewood we had gathered. Scared the crap out of me because they insist on using axes. Nonetheless, they did a great job.

Finally, there was an opportunity to play guitar. I unfolded my Furch fold-up guitar (an all-solid-wood little beauty made in the Czech Republic by a famous luthier). It brilliantly folds into a small backpack and is perfect for canoe trips, as well as for those plane trips so long ago pre-Covid. It has a great booming voice for its small size. The best fold-up or travel guitar I have ever had. Keegan joined me, he loves to sing, and Larry piped in once in a while—another person who loves to sing. I have waterproofed my songbooks, after

losing a few in rainy or wet conditions (well, one was in a hotel conference room in the Maritimes, but that is another story).

So, we sat in the chairs in the shallow water to keep the "no see ems" from biting my ankles. Every so often I check for leeches. We jammed a good hour or so. I never do this

too late to avoid bothering other campers across the lake at bedtime. Sound travels on these lakes forever. But it is always a canoe-trip tradition for us. (Heck, I will play anywhere for food.) Sometimes campsites across the lake even cheer us on. Other times passing canoes stop for a bit to listen to the tunes.

That night something ran by our tent in the middle of the night, quite frantic. Breathing hard. Running from something bigger, I suppose, but it never materialized. This is the "bear side" of Tom Thomson, and the bears here have learned to untie food barrels and knock them off tree branches like they did last August with the European tour group and the engineers camping beside us. They are getting smarter for sure, these black bears. But Larry and his sons have taken to hanging food barrels and sacks with a high new elaborate pulley and knotting system, one that passing canoeists have admired in previous years. We have never had an issue.

I woke early on the third day with stuff dropping onto my tent and the ground around us. I heard the squirrels chattering. "What are they doing up there?" Well, I was up and needed to go to the thunder box, then get coffee going. No one awoke to the aroma this time. I enjoyed the solitude and the snoring from the tents around me. A beautiful day in a beautiful place. Then a second visit to the thunder box and me messing with the bear bell that Ryan had tied to a string across the trail up to the thunder box got them up. I think I grunted like a bear too.

Another big breakfast, this time French toast, then cleanup. The day progressed slowly, naturally. I was finishing doing the dishes when Keegan called out, "Dad, Dad, I have a leech on me!" I bushwhacked over to him—there is a partial trail—and yes, he had a leech on his foot, quite engorged by the time I got there. Many years ago, when I was a camp counsellor in training on my first trip into Algonquin, the same thing happened to me. Several leeches had attached themselves. Our trip leader—Doug I think his name was—lit up a cigarette and briefly touched each of them, making them drop off without leaving their teeth embedded, which can cause nasty infections. This time Keegan was a little disconcerted since

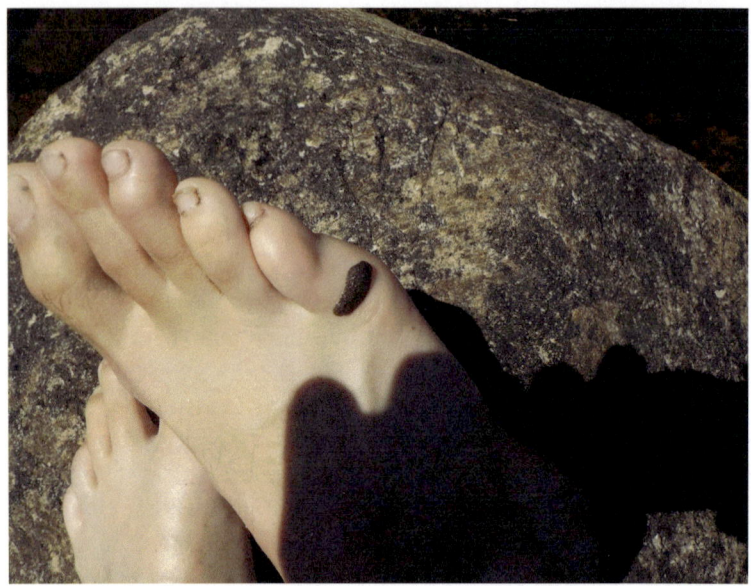

my aim with the cigarette was none too steady, but we succeeded, and Keegan and I then climbed into the canoe he had used to get to the point and continued exploring for wildlife. Of particular interest to him were spiders and snakes, which of course led to another earworm, a song from the seventies: "I don't like spiders and snakes, but if that's what it takes to love you"—or something like that!

We slowly examined every nook and cranny of the rock wall on one side of our bay and found some big spiders, but no snakes. We made our way over to an unoccupied campsite to check it out and brought back a large dry log. The guys were wondering where we were although we were quite visible.

Shortly after that, two canoes came over for a visit. Three guys and a young woman. It turned out they were all academics, either just finished their doctorates or in the process of doing so. The young woman was Canadian, from Edmonton, and the guys were from Mexico and Italy. We invited them ashore for some wine, and after a nice visit despite being in the middle of the pandemic, they left. We gave them the log Keegan and I found since they admitted they were not very experienced, this being the first canoe trip for three of them.

The young woman was in charge. Their paddling was not the strongest, but I admired their spirit of adventure. This park brings people from all over the world. I love it!

Then I decided it was time for the Camper of the Year Awards. I have always done this with the kids. Of course, everyone gets something. I'm not sure if I decided who was the best because these young men are all good at this now, and usually do one or two backcountry trips on their own each year. It pleases me immensely that Larry and I have passed this tradition onto them, hopefully to do with their own kids someday. I handed out small items that would be useful for their future backcountry endeavors.

At some point the boys took our table higher up the campsite to play cards. Larry ingeniously designed the table out of coroplast many years ago. It folds up into a canoeable package. Unfortunately, I left our other roll-up aluminum table in the car before we embarked. Larry reminded me of my transgression. It would have come in handy to provide more room for meal prep, eating and card playing.

At some point I went up to hang out with the kids for a minute, perhaps to take a photo, and sat down in my backpacking chair, which was all set up for me. But it was not steadily planted, and I promptly fell over backwards—it had nothing to do with my wine input, no—and I hit the food barrel whose top was open. Everything rolled down the hill, hitting my tent. No serious damage done. A few bruises I noticed later during my lovely post-trip shower at home.

Our last morning in the park, I woke to a huge thunderstorm before dawn. Lightning very bright, thunder overhead. Whenever it is like this, I think of my ancestors who fought for Canada in the first two world wars and what they must have gone through during artillery barrages!

Keegan was eager to go, as always. He pestered me the day before about leaving before the rest, who have a laid-back vibe and can take hours to decamp. We got to work and packed up quite quickly, another advantage of bringing the least amount of stuff in years thanks to my two backpacking trips, not to mention the ethos of Keegan's paddling gang from his high-school friend group who are minimalists!

Then to breakfast prep and consumption and clean-up. Larry asked me to wait. He likes it when we all paddle out together. Many times in the past, one of my boys had a work commitment so we had to leave a day beforehand. So, we waited, and waited, and waited. Finally, we set off in the early afternoon in good weather although there were menacing clouds to the northwest, very menacing ones. It is always so much lighter paddling out. We were no longer carrying eight or nine litres of wine in tetra paks. All gone. Our huge water jug also empty. And the small food barrel very light indeed. It makes such a difference. PLUS, we were paddling with the current as we headed toward the dam on Joe Lake.

We made fast progress, spurred on by the increasingly menacing clouds. Would it not be nice to get back, pack up the cars, and get to the Portage Store restaurant for our traditional delicious hamburger-and-fries-and-cold-beer meal before the skies opened up, or worse, thunder and lightning drove us to shore?

We shot over the beaver dam in one fell swoop, paddled down Littledoe and the Oxtongue and through Teepee, all quite calm. As we passed Joe Island on Joe Lake I heard someone we just passed call out "Mark!" Keegan and I stopped, and there was Alison, a very special PR executive I worked with in my early days in the business. She has done very well, now a senior executive vice-president in one of the top Canadian PR firms, and somehow recognized me with my Tilley hat and huge sunglasses! I met her husband for the first time and some friends of hers in another canoe; we chatted for a bit, and then they moved on, lots of paddling for them before nightfall. They said they were heading for Burnt Island Lake, which is one lake, a long river, and two nasty portages away.

Almost in the same spot many years ago we ran into a character in a kayak, very well-tanned, in a small bathing suit, lean and muscled, looking quite wild. He turned out to be a former brother-in-law of mine. He had split up with my sister-in-law and this was where he came to heal. He had found a site on Joe Lake, up high, accessible only by a steep staircase, which I have never found again. He also found a basketball which he named "Wilson," built a net, and was literally on the lam. Somehow the wardens had not caught him but he had been there for weeks, only paddling down Canoe Lake to the Portage Store for supplies. We stayed that night at his site, Larry and I and our boys. My boys never forgot that experience, "Wilson" and the net and Glenn living relatively wild. I imagine the wardens have to deal with this kind of thing more than we think.

We blew through the portage quite quickly, hurried on by the pending storm, which unleashed on us just as we pushed off down the small river from the dam, our portage cheat. We had enough warning to get ponchos on, however. It poured the whole way. Canoe Lake almost always is mean to me (and more particularly to my daughter), with winds almost always against us, storms, rain…. To be sure, it has been calm a few times, and then it is lovely. This trip back was still eerie, no campers at either Ahmek or Wapomeo.

One year our resident MacGyver, Larry, figured a way to create a massive sail out of a large tarp. We lashed the canoes together and sailed southbound on Canoe Lake, cutting the trip to about 15 minutes. Now that was a fun ride!

This paddle, however, was not. We got soaked. Cold. We finally landed at the beach, got our vehicles, and loaded the sodden gear and canoes. Thankfully, I had remembered to put a dry set of clothes in my car for this very eventuality and changed in the shower hut before joining everyone in the restaurant. The only thing I forgot to bring was another pair of shoes, so I was still in my soaked water shoes.

We had a simple meal, but so gooood, as always. A cold beer. Hamburger. Salad, fries. I remember when my son Hunter was young—after one of our canoe trips he fell asleep eating such a meal, a smile on his face.

Then off we went, in the opposite direction down Highway 60 than the rest of the group. I promised to drop off copies of *The Broken Ukulele*, the prequel to this book, at the Opeongo store, roughly in the middle of the park, on the largest lake in the park. The manager of the store kindly agreed to take some books to sell. Thrilling for a struggling author such as myself. While there, I bought a dry pair of Crocs water shoes; my feet were becoming cold and waterlogged. Keegan was not thrilled to add another hour to our trip home but promptly fell asleep as I turned right back onto Highway 60 and eventually home.

One last memory about Lake Opeongo. Years ago, one of us had a cancer scare, so Larry generously rented a boat service that took us up this huge and very dangerous lake toward the north end of the park. We stayed on Bear Island, which was ironic since Larry has a healthy fear of bears. He usually has several canisters of bear spray readily available in our campsites and on his person. This time he decided to test one of the sprays in the woods, away from our campsite. The wind blew the spray directly back into his and his son's faces. They came out of the woods yelling and dove into the water fully clothed to get it off. Years later, I inadvertently set off some bear spray in my home office, which caused havoc in the household at the time and again for my dear colleagues when they helped pack up said office.

That trip, we explored the lake's north end, where there are beach campsites. The aforementioned Roy MacGregor told me once that one of his favourite places in the park runs north from there up the Crow River into Little and Big Crow Lakes, where there are some last surviving old-growth pines.

But back to *this* trip. It had been so nice to spend time with my son Keegan whom I have not seen much during the pandemic, thanks to the quarantines. I loved our few hours together looking for spiders and snakes. It reminded me so much of him when he was small and fascinated by such things. Later, when I unpacked everything in the garage, a very big spider came out of one of the packs and wandered across the garage floor, never to be seen again. I hope it has not found its way into the house but instead has found a home in my garage!

On the way home Keegan asked me shyly what songs I kept humming on the trip. I've already mentioned "Sundown," but also had McCartney's "Band on the Run" and the aforementioned Dire Straits' "Money for Nothing"—the "MTV song"—going through my head.

When you are camping with a big, busy group there is not much time alone, hence not too much time to think, except when you are at the thunder box, or scouting for dead trees, or off on a paddle by yourself. But it was wonderful as always to be with my best friend since high school, Larry. He still makes me laugh, despite my PR company dying a nasty death thanks to Covid, my sad state of financial affairs, my lack of a partner in life.

And of course, this beautiful Algonquin Park to come back to one or twice or thrice a year. What a gift was given us. What a humble Canadian blend of stewardship, and balance, and sustainability. What a legacy for our grandchildren, our great grandchildren, for the many visitors from around the world. Please support this place always.

And to be with all of these boys we have taken on so many trips. It's priceless. To see how they have grown up, made lives and careers for themselves. Some have found life mates already, others have been heartbroken but will try again, and as I mentioned earlier, they are doing their own backcountry trips now. And they still even invite me to come along!

An important romantic relationship for me ended during Covid, one I restarted from my younger days. I will keep her name private but felt terrible about it. However, it was not workable on several levels. But I thought about her several times on this trip, and in the little time I had to palaver with Larry, he encouraged me to reach out and again say I was sorry, which I did some months after this trip.

I have never taken a love interest on a backcountry canoe or backpacking trip. This is something I hope to achieve before I can no longer do this wonderful, simple thing of getting into a canoe and paddling in this beautiful place.

But maybe the next Algonquin adventure, by bike—"bikepacking" it's called—will be solo, just because none of my usual backcountry pals seem very enthused about it! Talk about minimalism, fitting everything onto a bike! However, I may be able to convince Larry, who is an avid mountain biker. Or maybe some wonderful woman will join me. I wonder what I will forget and break next time! What simple, beautiful things await. What the morrow brings.

About the Author

Mark Hunter LaVigne took this selfie on his solo backpacking trip to Maple Leaf Lake in Algonquin Park.

He is the author or co-author of six books: *The Adventures of Matilda the Tooth Fairy*; *Fundamentals of Public Relations and Marketing Communications*; *In the News* (third edition); *Proactive Media Relations: A Canadian Perspective*; *The Broken Ukulele*; and the present volume.

He is also a songwriter and performer on guitar, ukulele, harmonica and vocals. He wrote four of the eight songs on *Out of the Woods*, by The Coyotes, and has an EP ready for release with some more of his songs. He likes to put them under the Christmas tree for his loved ones.

He lives in Aurora, Ontario with a few of his grown children, and his buddy cat Simba.

Made in the USA
Monee, IL
04 May 2026